MW01181076

Flights on the Wind

Text by Ed Gray

Artwork by Brett Smith

WILLOW CREEK PRESS
Minocqua, Wisconsin

Published by
Willow Creek Press
P.O. Box 147
Minocqua, Wisconsin 54548

Editor: Andrea Donner
Design: Katrin Wooley

Library of Congress Cataloging-in-Publication

Gray, Ed, 1945-
Flights on the wind / text by Ed Gray ; artwork by Brett Smith.
p. cm.
ISBN 1-57223-209-9 (Hardcover : alk. paper)
1. Waterfowl shooting. I. Smith, Brett, 1958- II. Title.
SK331.G74 2003
799.2'44--dc21

Printed in Canada 2003011405

For Bunny Burnes, gone now, never to be forgotten.

Here's hoping you finally found all the bluebills.

TABLE OF CONTENTS

Chapter One

Promise

A lifetime of waterfowling spins itself out much like each of the seasons that mark it, skylarking in the easy warmth of its beginning, slowly gathering focus and intensity as the weather hardens and the flights increase, and ending unpredictably, somewhere later, somewhere colder, somewhere darker, when all the birds are gone.

I say this from long experience, though not all of it my own. For me, the flights are still on, the birds are still coming down from the north; the weather is colder but deep snow and full ice-over won't be here tomorrow, or even the next day; darkness isn't yet a factor. It's still shooting light, and I expect it's going to be for a while to come. But a season is a season and a lifetime is a lifetime: You can't live either one fully without knowing that it's going to end.

Or knowing where it began. A lifetime of fowling doesn't necessarily start the first time someone hands you a shotgun, or even on the day you shoot your first bird. It starts — not the gunning, but the *life* of gunning — when you realize that this is not just something you like and may do again: This is something that you love and *will* do again. More than that, even: This is something that you will not go through life *without* doing. That realization may come on slowly, so slowly in fact that it may pass without your noting it, the way newly-falling flakes become a snowdrift. When did the growing pile become a drift? With which individual flake? When did you become a waterfowler? On which particular hunt?

I think I know, although I didn't have an inkling at the time. I didn't know it yet because that hunt was just the catalyst, the flicker of the butterfly's wing in the Amazon that spins fractally outward through the weather, spawning snow-laden cold fronts in New England. The ones that would call me and Becky, our children and our dogs, good friends and people we didn't even know, out onto salt marshes, backwater sloughs, and frozen rivers for the next quarter century — and beyond.

The day in question, the one on which that figurative swallowtail flapped its wings, happened on a salt marsh in Ipswich,

Massachusetts, on opening day of the coastal waterfowl season twenty-three years ago.

It was the middle of October, and a thick coastal fog had rolled in off the cold ocean water on the other side of the uninhabited barrier beach that separated the marsh from the rolling destruction of the three- and four-day nor'easters that surged against the coast every winter, the hard winds and pounding surf that dissipated their energy against the uplifted dunes of the barrier island and re-sculpted the mile of sand into newly-formed abstracts of drifting French curves and wind-bent grasses.

The fog had come in sometime after midnight, when I had stepped out onto my salt-weathered back deck and looked up at the night sky, listening for gabbling black ducks out in the dark while my golden retriever Casey trotted across the small patch of mowed grass to get closer to the edge of the tide line, pulling in marsh scents and listening for the same sounds. Out in the open bay water of the estuary, a half-mile away, a goose honked, answered a few seconds later by another. Casey's ears went up, and then he trotted back beside me, sitting and staring in the direction from which the calls had come. Like every dog

I've owned since, he was as ready to hunt in the middle of the night, or in the middle of a back yard, or in the back of a Jeep, as he was in a place where it might actually happen. Good hunting dogs have so many unspoken lessons for us, this one among them — one could do worse than to be always ready.

But at that point in his short life, Casey hadn't yet retrieved a goose or a duck. Tonight he was reacting purely on instinct, breeding, and whatever had brushed itself into his memory over the three months we had just spent together on the marsh, which tomorrow we would both hunt for the first time. He was just a year old and I was thirty-one.

"Come on, Casey," I said, waiting until he came over and then scratching his ears. "Tomorrow it counts."

In the morning, I knew as soon as I got up that we were in trouble. The fog was as thick as it gets; ducks would be loathe to fly in it and the geese absolutely would not. But Casey knew none of this — he just wanted to go. What could I say to him? What could I say to myself? It was opening day.

Our house in those years sat on the edge of a small wooded island on the inland side of the marsh; our driveway was a gravel two-track that at its low point went completely under water once a month on the moon tides, when the entire marsh flooded into a saltwater lake and our half-acre of high ground truly became an island. But this month's big tide was two weeks away from that opening day, so Casey and I could — and did — walk out the basement storm door, across the ragged strip of lawn, and directly onto the marsh itself. It was an hour before dawn, black as pitch and, because I had left no lights on behind us, immediately disorienting. Fifty yards onto the marsh Casey and I were perfectly enveloped in night fog. Following the path we had worn on the grassy marsh top and winding our way carefully past the natural channels and mosquito-control trenches that had been dug in the 1930s, the dog and I worked our way slowly out toward the setup spot I had already selected.

I had selected the spot in September, a couple of months after Becky and I had moved into the house on the island and had begun to learn our way around the mile-wide marsh that surrounded it. Deer were the key, regularly crossing from the farm fields on the south side to the other island, an impenetrably-vegetated hillock of high ground further out in the marsh, closer to the mouth of the river; their route, well-worn by generations of whitetails, was the one path across that avoided all of the ditches and we used it too, gaining dry-footed access through the maze of ditches and channels to the very center of the marsh. That's where I had decided to set up the opening day blind that Casey and I were going to use this morning. If we could find it. The deer path was a good route, but first we had to get to it, and now all of my visual clues were gone.

But Casey knew the way. His clues weren't visual; they were olfactory. He just put his nose down and trotted ahead as if the fog wasn't even there and I trotted along behind him. Sort of — I had a sack of decoys over one shoulder and a shotgun in my other hand.

"Casey," I hissed at him when he got too far ahead, keeping my voice low. "*Sssittt!*" In a few steps I'd find him, sitting at the command and waiting to be turned loose for his next guide-dog leg. It took twenty minutes instead of our usual ten, but eventually we found the spot, a bend in one of the natural tidal creeks where it intersected with another, forming a twenty-yard-across pocket that held some water even at low tide, nine or ten feet down from the grassy top where Casey and I knew stood in the fog.

"Sit, Casey. Stay," I said. He did and then I slid down the steep, dank-mudded bank into the knee-deep water to set out my decoys: seven cork-bodied magnums — five black ducks and a pair of Canadas. I had read somewhere that an odd number was good for ducks, indicating to a single that this group wasn't paired up, a theory that requires, of course, that ducks be able to count. Maybe they can, maybe they can't; no one can really know, but why not allow for it? Pascal's Wager in the duck marsh, right, Casey?

He whimpered as I tossed out the last of the blocks, wanting even still to go get it, after almost a year of training that said *no, not the decoys, no, not the decoys, no, not the decoys...* Casey still wanted the decoys. Or, like all the good ones, anything else that hit the water in front of him. You could still fool him with a balled-up handful of wet sand.

I clambered back up the mudbank, slipping and grabbing a tuft of spartina grass to keep from sliding all the way back down. "Good boy," I whispered. "Ssshhh."

I gathered the bag and my shotgun, then moved to the matted depression in the tall grass that I had made two evenings before, when I had brought Casey out here to watch the ducks come in at dark, circling overhead before dropping in like oversized bats on cupped wings, splashing down into the half-filled creek right in front of us while I held the dog in check, teaching him to stay quiet even as he nearly exploded with the desire to get them. In the past month we had done this eight or ten times, getting ready for this morning. Now here we were, and we were ready. But we were also in the fog. "I don't know, Casey," I whispered. "We could be here a while."

An hour later nothing had happened. Gradually it had grown toward daylight, a gathering brightness that came without definition and increasing so slowly that there seemed from minute to minute to be no change at all. And then, as if it had always been that way but I was just now noticing it, it would be brighter. Just slightly brighter, but more light nonetheless. I looked at my watch: legal shooting time had come and gone by fifteen minutes.

"Now I do know, Casey," I said. "We are going to be here for a while."

I'd like to say that Casey whimpered or whined in disappointment, but I can't. Another of his lessons. He just sat beside me on the grass, looking at me when I spoke and looking away when I was quiet.

"You know, Casey," I said. "We're going to be doing this again. We're going to be doing it a lot."

Below us in the creek, there was a faint gurgle as the incoming tide began to trickle past, shifting the decoys.

"We're going to do it here. And we're going to do it in a lot of other places. We might even go so far you'll have to get in an airplane to do it."

Casey perked up. Down in the creek the decoys were moving steadily now.

"And we won't always be alone like this either," I said. "Fact, most of the time we won't. Becky will be here almost always. And sometimes Larry and Reed and John. And others. And you better be ready for this: other dogs."

Casey turned and looked at me, letting his tongue out and panting. Then he closed up again and turned toward what little there was of the wind, holding his nose up and into it, sampling.

Tell me about it, he said.

Well, in my mind he did. At least I think he did. In my memory of it today he did. And in my memory of it today, I know I did. I started to tell him about it. I started to tell him all about it. And that has taken a long time. So long, in fact, that I'm still doing it.

Chapter Two

The Canadas of Ipswich

In late October we'd start to listen for the geese. Just before we went to bed, I'd go out on the porch with the dog to see if they were in yet; together we'd stand there, peering into the dark distance across the marsh and waiting for the muted *ho-onk*. If the wind was from the north, and if the birds were there, we'd hear it soon enough.

Later in the season, when the big flocks had all come down, you could hear them every night, but here in the early season, when we were waiting for the first arrivals, it wasn't so certain. Casey would sniff about in the dried grasses at the edge of the marsh and I'd stand there quietly, hearing only the raspy calls and feeding chuckles of the black ducks gathered on the tidal flats. Our second year there set the pattern. The night before, we'd heard nothing so Becky and I went out in the morning to the black duck blind, setting up for a pass shot or two at the birds as they headed inland to the still-open fresh water. The ducks flew early, sporadically and high, and we had no shots. Another quiet morning, it seemed, and we stood up to walk home.

Ho-onk! From the flats, just out of sight, 200 yards away. The first northern birds were in. We knew what to do; we'd learned it the hard way the year before. Staying low, we separated; Becky moved 100 yards down the creek, Casey and I stayed put. We waited.

We waited a half hour. There was no one else on the marsh, the birds hadn't yet been shot at, and they weren't going to move until they were ready. There would be plenty of warning when they got ready.

It started with an isolated honk from one of the still-unseen birds. An answering call or two, then quiet again. A few minutes later, another honk, and a chorus of answers. There was no wind, and we could hear them loosening up, five-foot wingspans drumming the morning air, the sound coming to us like parade ground flags caught in a gusty wind. Silence again, and then they came.

They must have been working themselves into position on the water, because they came up in a line, 150 birds fanned out across 300 yards of marsh, and they were up in a rush of pure sound.

The sound of it. We'd still hear it, out on the marsh, walking in March or September; we'd come to the spot where we crouched that day and the sound would still be there, lingering in the salt air. A quick roar of wings like a breaking wave, and the honking calls all together in one long, two-toned peal, rising and spreading in front of us.

For three seconds we couldn't see them, and then they were in sight, coming over the crest of the marsh, winging easily now. Coming right at us, 200 yards away. The dog was transfixed.

I looked to the left, saw that Becky was down, ready, and that the line of geese would pass over her spot. So I put my chin on my knees and waited. The birds came on, and then they were there — fifty yards out, thirty yards up. I sat up, brought the gun to my shoulder, swung through the bird directly in front of me, and fired as the barrels blotted out his head. Nothing. I held the lead steady and shot again. The goose fell out of the air like his support string had been cut, and when the bird hit the marsh in front of me, Casey didn't need any hand signals — he was off.

I hadn't heard Becky shoot, and I turned that way in time to see her hurriedly ejecting spent shells. The geese were still above her, passing quickly, and then one of them faltered behind her, and fell. I pointed at it and shouted, and Becky turned in time to see it land in the grasses 100 yards away.

It was a great moment. The first geese of the year, Becky's first goose ever, and Casey's introduction to the art of retrieving a ten-pound gamebird. My memory of it is continuous and very clear, but I have stop-action images in my mind:

Becky standing on the marsh after watching the bird go down, pointing to herself and silently saying, "Me?"; Casey trying to get a grip on the goose, whining a bit in frustration and finally taking a tenuous hold of a wing near the shoulder and dragging it fifty yards to where I waited; and overlaying it all is the slowly diminishing, steady calling of the geese as they faded into the brightening eastern sky.

It wasn't always that way, of course. Not even close. We'd try to get out every day in the season, but we rarely had the place to ourselves, especially in the late season when the big birds were out there every morning. The marsh is big, and the geese always took off into the wind — unless there was a bit of east in it, they wouldn't come our way. And after they'd heard the guns a few times they'd learn to take some altitude before they crossed the marsh, and they left the flats earlier every day so that by late in the season there weren't many of them around in the daylight. We'd call it a good season if we took a half dozen.

Black ducks were the mainstay of our season on the marsh. They were there more often, trading in and out of the marsh all day, and the shooting was usually over decoys. It was something to see them circle carefully and then commit with cupped wings, seventy yards out and coming into the set, and the dog work could be spectacular on a good day.

But when we looked back across each of those seasons, feet up and lounging in a warm place, counting the days until next opening day, it was the geese that led the parade of memories. I'm not really sure why this was.

It may be that a goose is big game, a true trophy of waterfowling. It may be the grace of the bird itself, or it may be the rarity of actually hitting one. As Reed says, when he shoots he expects a duck to fall, he's surprised when a grouse comes down, but a goose — a goose is a miracle.

Probably it's all of these things, but at the top of my list is what I still hear when I close my eyes, even after all these years.

I hear the sudden call of a single goose, coming clearly to me from an unseen place on a cold morning in November. Like a single chime from the clock tower it marks the beginning of a long afternoon, pointing toward darkness but promising much ringing before sunset.

Chapter Three

Jump Shooting

When I couldn't find the thing last fall, I went to the catalogs, looking for a new duck strap.

I didn't find it there, either. Not even the skinny little belt-loop kind you hang quail on. I'd have settled for that, even though what I really wanted was one of those wide, shoulder-hung double-enders that can balance three or four puddle ducks on your chest against a butt-bumping Canada goose draped down your back.

Well, it *had* been a couple of years since I'd been jump-shooting, but it hadn't occurred to me that everyone else had quit, too. How about you? When was the last time you slipped on a pair of hip boots, crooked your duck gun, pocketed a handful of shells, and hiked out across the big marsh to look for a bird or two that were already there?

Yeah, me too, I guess. More than a couple years, on reflection. Make you this deal: You find me a good, heavy-duty game strap, and I'll take you to the salt marsh. We'll go in November, around Thanksgiving. I'll check the tide tables to find us a good morning, one with a dawn flood to bring the birds well up into the marsh and hold them there for the next couple hours while the water drops. Around nine or ten we'll start, as soon as the tide's down five or six feet and the birds are all down in the creeks and drainage ditches. That's when we'll sneak them.

Civilized, isn't it? Starting a duck hunt at midmorning? That's the first pleasant surprise that jump-shooting brings, but it's certainly not the best.

For one thing, we'll stay warm. No motionless crouching in single-digit wind-chills today; this one's a hike, and an into-the-wind one at that. You're going to burn some calories.

We'll start at the east end, for no other reason other than to let the dog burn a few calories of his own. Since we're conjuring this one anyway, why don't we bring my old golden retriever, Casey? He loved jump-shooting more than any dog that ever hunted with me, and he's always right nearby whenever I think about it. Won't take a second to call him over.

There. Ready. Yeah, that was a hand signal. Casey and I worked that out back then, in those years when we lived near here and worked this marsh every week. Didn't help the stealth any to be shouting at the dog, so I taught Casey to sit, stay, and come to specific hand signals.

Stop here. I'll show you where we're going to go, since we won't be doing any talking out there close to the birds.

We'll start by the edge of that big creek. There's a widening there that you can't see til you're almost on top of it, and it holds calm water right through low tide. If there are ducks on the marsh today, the best bet is to look there first. In jump-shooting, you definitely do not save the best for last; your first shot's going to move birds, so you ought to be in position when they go.

We'll approach the creek about thirty yards apart, walking. About ten yards from the edge, I'll show Casey the flat of my hand and he'll sit; than we'll go the rest of the way in a low crouch. Remember — the water's six feet below the edge, well out of the wind, so if you see a disturbed surface, get ready. Ripples mean ducks. Crouch low, move slow; hold the gun lightly. One more step…

Eruption.

White water and green heads; flying spray and beating wings.

Guns up and seeking, seeking. Pointing. Shooting. Shooting again. You're a quick shot if you can dump one back into the creek. More likely there will be a bird or two down on the other side, up at our own level in the marsh grass with the muddy creek between.

That's okay. That's what the dog's for, the quivering golden retriever ten yards behind us.

"Fetch 'em up, Casey."

Now, while the dog's rooting around over there, you might reach into your coat pocket and dig out that duck strap you brought.

In a morning's jump-shooting, we'll make a half dozen approaches. Maybe one will pay off. Most of them will show no ducks at all. And at least once we'll creep carefully up, peer into the creek, and see ducks — seventy yards to our right, necks straight and bodies frozen, staring back at us.

Another eruption. Way down there.

Drop flat on your back immediately. Chances are they didn't all see you, and they're going to come up out of the creek not knowing where the problem is. Some may come our way. Maybe. But not usually.

One time, between the two open portions of the coastal split season on this marsh, I went out alone with a camera. Out in the middle of the marsh, at very low tide, I had to cross one of these creeks. I hadn't seen a duck all morning, but I was certain they were here somewhere. Down in the winding creek I worked my way around a bend, looking for a shallow place to cross, and there I came upon two black ducks swimming around the corner toward me. They bolted upward and, instead of trying for a picture, I threw myself back against the creek bank out of old habit.

That's when the *other* black ducks got up. In a cloud. In a roaring, milling, quacking cloud of two hundred or more. I was transfixed as they swirled around and past me, lifting like

smoke out of the creek to fan out and away, crossing and circling the marsh as they climbed and mixed into ragged bands in the sky. I stayed low and watched them try to regroup out over the dunes of the barrier beach, and I hunkered even lower as I began to realize that they weren't going to leave.

They wanted to come back.

And they did. In pairs and small groups for the next hour, the birds came back into the creek, circling high and decoying down, gliding in with cupped wings and splayed feet as I took their pictures from my hunkering place in the grassy creek bank.

I shot the whole roll of film at them, quietly clicking, and then tried to just as quietly sneak away.

Not a chance. When they left this time, they left.

Back in those years, Becky and I lived in a rented house right on the edge of that marsh, and we gunned it almost every day in the season, slipping out at dawn for the odd pass shot at the geese getting up from their nightly stay in the river estuary. When the tide was right, we'd set up for ducks with decoys on the far side, and once or twice a week, we'd go jump-shooting along the creeks. With that many permutations available, we began to mix and match.

If I planned to make a half-day jump of it, I'd slip a plastic decoy onto each end of the duck strap and slip my call lanyard around my neck. Didn't add much weight, and if I then wanted to, I could make a quick setup somewhere out there. In reality, it was a foolproof way to talk myself into a little nap. Two miles from the house on a quiet afternoon, I'd toss out the dekes, get Casey to lie down beside me, close my eyes, and trust him to start shaking if anything interesting flew near.

But whether you take the Carry-Lites or not, don't ever leave the calls behind, even on a pure jump-shoot. One morning I crept up to one of my good creek bends just in time to see a hen mallard turning the corner, swimming away from me, unspooked. The creek widened where the bird went, and there was no way to sneak closer without being seen. So I signaled in the dog, got down low, and waited to see if she'd swim back. Around the corner, the bird quacked instead, once, low. I pulled out my call and quacked back, once, trying to imitate.

Quack. Quack. From around the corner.

"Quack. Quack."" I answered.

Pause.

Quack. Quack. Quack.

Okay, I thought. Why not? "Quack. Quack. Quack."

Pause. And then the watery rush of lifting duck wings, silenced quickly as the mallard banked on cupped wings right toward me.

Casey was impressed.

Walking up the ducks. In the four years we lived there, it became as seasonally constant and natural to us as picking October apples or casting for June stripers in the same creeks. Our daughter Hope was in the third grade during one of those duck seasons, and one Saturday afternoon she was due at a classmate's birthday party. Becky had got her dressed up for it and was almost out the door to the car when I saw the two black ducks close in. It was from the living room window, the one that looked out across the marsh, and the two birds came straight into the closest creek of them all, less than fifty yards from the house.

"You got a minute?" I called to Becky.

"No," she answered from the opened front door.

"Okay. I'll get these two myself."

Pause.

Becky appeared beside me at the window. "What two?"

Fifteen minutes later, as I sat on the porch picking the two ducks — the one I had taken going right and the one she had taken going left — Becky dropped Hope at the birthday party. They were only a little late, and Becky still had on the camouflage parka she'd thrown on for the quick stalk. As she bent over to straighten the bow on the back of Hope's party dress, a couple of high-brass number fives fell out the pocket onto the floor in front of the other mommies, most of whom had on party dresses, too. At least by comparison to Becky.

Silence in the room. Becky nonchalantly picked up the shells, put them in her pocket, and brushed back her fallen hair. There was marsh mud streaked on her hand, and just a trace of duck blood. They were all staring at her.

"Oh, it's nothing," she said. "Nothing. I was just out doing a little jump shooting."

Chapter Four

Bunny

Sandy Neck is a mile-long scrub island on the south side of Cape Cod, low and uninhabitable, separated from the mainland and the summer houses that overlook it only by a winding saltwater channel that isn't 100 yards at its widest point. In July and August the channel is busy with small boats and packed on its north shore with seasonal docks and the varied craft kept tied up to them, and the island itself is busy on its edges with beach-goers and shell-seekers. But the interior dunes are pretty much left to the birds, the hardy beach roses and waving grasses, and the poison ivy that keeps most of the sun-bathers down near the high-tide line. In the late fall, of course, all but the grasses and the barren rose bushes are gone; even most of the birds have left, leaving the neck and its two small tidal inlets open, quiet and available to the migrating black ducks. They arrive in November, right about Thanksgiving. At least they used to — I haven't been there in a while. Not since Kenny Burnes and I used to hunt it twenty-five years ago, sometimes just the two of us, other times with his brother Danny and his father, the unsuitably-named Bunny, a man who was nobody's prey species.

The Burnes' lived in one of the big summer houses overlooking Sandy Neck, a rambling old ark of a home with salt-weathered cedar shingles on the outside and a New England-style kitchen the size of a small meeting room on the inside. Above the kitchen sink was a window with an unobstructed view of the best of the Neck's lagoons, the one Bunny had gunned with his own father long before Kenny and Danny were born. The procedure was time-honored: I'd arrive at the house in the dark, an hour or so before legal shooting time and go quietly through the unlocked front door, down the main entrance hall, through the dining room and into the kitchen, gathering tail-thumping Labrador retrievers as I went. The dogs knew what was up and were more than ready, but like the hunters already gathered in the coffee-brewing kitchen, they knew also to keep quiet. Any number of Burnes' would be still asleep upstairs, three generations of them if

Kenny's wife Barbara had come down with him this weekend and brought the kids. None were old enough yet to hunt. In the kitchen we'd fill Thermoses with coffee, then slip out the back door with the dogs, carrying our guns and waders down to the dock where we'd get into a Boston Whaler and idle across the channel to the lagoon. The blinds were already built — we'd done that in October, digging sand pits above the high-tide line, then weaving dune grasses and driftwood around the edges — and the decoys were already cached in burlap bags, ready to be set. From the time we left the dock, it only took twenty minutes to be rigged, hidden and ready.

On the day in question it was Bunny, Kenny, Danny, and me, and we hurried a bit. The skies were clear and dawn would come early and fast. So would the blacks ducks, winging low from the south, somewhere out in Nantucket Sound, doing whatever it was that black ducks do at night. Resting, we always assumed, rafted together in small groups just offshore where the land-based night predators couldn't reach them. We'd seen red foxes and raccoons on the island. At first light, we knew, the ducks would begin to come back into the lagoon, wanting to spend the daylight in this quiet place of shallow water, eel grass, and small crustaceans. Kenny and I set out the decoys while Bunny and Danny cleared blown sand from the two pits, ten yards away from each other at a small bend in the lagoon. The two blinds angled away from each other so that each one had a clear and non-competing view of half the lagoon; Kenny and I got into one and Danny and his father in the other. And then we waited. It was the week before Thanksgiving and the second half of the Massachusetts coastal split season had been open only for two days. On none of them had anyone been in here: On Sandy Neck, at least, this was opening day.

The first bunch came quietly, and in a wave. It was ten minutes before legal shooting time, not even light enough to see them coming, gliding toward us in a spread-out line before they canted their wings in unison, braking in the air just across the lagoon, a hundred yards away and only ten feet off the water. We heard them then, the sudden stalling rush of air through thirty sets of cupped wings followed almost instantly by the magnified *whoosh!* of displaced water as they all set down in the middle of the lagoon.

None of us moved. None of us could. The

birds were on the water, fifty yards in front of us, unaware we were here. In the dark we could barely make them out against the far shoreline. They began to move about, staying in the center of the lagoon, still wary and not at all settled down. In my mind I could already hear the sudden sound of them going, bursting skyward and showering away, downwind and gone. But they didn't. In the lagoon, and in the blind where I hunkered with Kenny, it was silent.

"There must be thirty of them!" he hissed. "Thirty! I've never *seen* that many come in here."

I didn't answer; there was no need to. If Kenny had never seen that many here, I certainly hadn't. Bunny must have, though, I

thought, back in the forties or fifties, when he'd been there in the heydays, when he'd seen them all. "Where are the bluebills?" he would rasp several times each season. "There used to be so many." But he never complained about the black ducks. They were still here, and even if there weren't as many, there were plenty. We only wanted two or three even on the good days, when we could have limited in the first half hour. Today we could limit on the first volley, as soon as we stood up and spooked them into the air.

"We can't shoot," whispered Kenny.

"Not yet," I agreed.

"I mean not at *all*. Not this many. The ones that get away will never come back. We need to move them out quietly, so they'll come back in two's and three's."

He was right. This bunch might be all of them, all the birds that had rafted together out in the Sound last night. If we wanted to hunt for more than the first fifteen seconds of legal light, we'd have to ease them out, then work the small groups that would filter back in. But what if they didn't? What if we spooked them just as thoroughly by easing them out as we would if we stood up and shot two or three of them? These birds were here, as good as in the hand. Why not wait till good light, stand up, let them get off the water, shoot one or two apiece and be happy? Silently in my mind I continued the debate, answering my own questions:

Because you hunt for the hunt, not just for the quarry. Right?

Right.

Right. That's why.

Fine, but answer me this.

Okay.

How do you eat the hunt, not just the quarry? What's your recipe for that?

The same as yours. You've already got it.

Yeah? What's that?

You re-live it. You remember it. You play the hunt over. Just like you always do.

Oh.

Just like you're already doing with this one.

I am? How do you know that?

What do you mean 'How do I know that?' I'm you.

Sometimes I wonder.

"What?" hissed Kenny.

"Nothing," I whispered back.

"Well stay down," he said. "I'm going to move them out before it's too late."

I knew what he meant. In another few minutes it would be close enough to legal so that Danny or Bunny might shoot when the birds got up. Without saying anything else, Kenny propped his gun in the corner of the blind, crept out the back and began a low crawl in the sand, moving to the left, away from the other blind. When he got ten yards away, he stopped and tentatively lifted a hand. Nothing happened. He waved his hand. Nothing happened. He waved it harder.

Quack! One of the black ducks lifted up with a quick splash and started winging away, startled and fast. There was one second of frozen silence before…

Wha-oo-oo-sh-shshshsh! All the rest of them left in a clattering bunch, winging directly away, following the one that had seen Kenny's hand waving in the grass.

"Oh no!" said Bunny over in the other blind. "Who moved?"

"Shhh," whispered Kenny, crawling quickly back in with me. "Don't let him know!"

"Oh no!" said Bunny again. "Did you *see* them? Did you see how *many*? Oh no."

"They'll be back," answered Kenny, keeping his voice as low as he could. "I don't think they're spooked."

"Not *spooked*?" croaked Bunny back. "Not spooked? They left like bats out of hell, that's how not spooked they were!"

"Shhh," said Kenny. "Some of them might be coming back already."

"Fat chance," mumbled Bunny, quieting down. "Oh, but did you just *see* them? Have you ever seen so many in one bunch?"

"It's okay, Dad," I could just hear Danny say, whispering in the other blind. "It's okay. They'll be back." I suspected that Danny knew what his brother had done. Or at least what one of us over here had done.

Bunny quieted down. "Oh, but didn't you just see them," he kept mumbling, growing quieter and quieter. "Have you never seen anything so beautiful? Have you never?"

I had never. And as the lagoon once again grew quiet and each of the four of us did the same, I wondered if I ever would again.

Chapter Five

Larry

Because bird hunting these days seems to be more and more alluring to anyone with a spare weekend, a credit card, and his name on a catalog mailing list, I thought you should get to know Larry, a guy whose one-owner pump gun predates the Korean War.

Before he moved to Texas, you could find him on any number of New England salt marshes, wood duck ponds, or pit blinds, pretty much any morning from October on through the bonus late-season coastal goose fiasco. These days he gets back only once or twice a season, but his pattern hasn't changed. He'll be out there alone, or in a group of his DU pals, but you'll have no trouble picking him out: Larry will be the one with the brown gun and the old army coat, lugging ammo cans and looking like one of those spectral lost guerrillas who never got the word that the war ended.

Where you won't find him, of course, is anywhere near a retail outfitter or gun shop. Larry views bird hunting not as a sport or pastime, but as an integral part of his day-to-day existence, a spiritual and cultural overlay to his well-tempered view of the world as a place where a person ought to make his own way. Or, as he usually puts it: "Have you seen what they're charging for this stuff these days?"

He says this all the time, unchanged and mantra-like. The first time I heard it was a couple of decades ago in his basement, after the first time I went goose hunting with him on Cape Cod. We had a half-dozen big Canadas to pick and it was too cold to do it outside, so we were down by the furnace, carefully pulling away the outside breast feathers so that we could then — and even more carefully — lift the down and drop it into Larry's green plastic bags.

"If you pick it dry," he was saying, "and keep it that way, it'll be just as good as anything from Eddie Bauer. I make my own down coats. Just start with a nylon shell, sew an old chamois shirt to the inside and pack the middle with this down. Works great."

He kept picking. "Good on sleeping bags, too."

"Hmm." I said. "Kinda complicated, isn't it? Sewing in those angled baffles and all?"

Larry looked up at me, made a "say what?" face.

"You know," I answered. "To keep the loft."

He waved it off, went back to picking. "Ahh, that's hype," he said.

The next time we went out I paid a little more attention to what Larry wore and, sure enough, there was his homemade parka: an ancient softball warm-up jacket packed full of goose feathers that he put on under his rubberized camouflage poncho. A few wisps of unbleached down fluttered out as he shrugged his way into the outfit, and I realized that I'd noticed them before, on other hunts, but had assumed they were just the usual lost plumage from an earlier day's bag, like the random detritus that drops out of your shooting vest's game pouch late in the season.

Wrong. The feathers weren't from the birds; they were from Larry. He wasn't exactly a lock-stitch seamster, and then there was the problem of the aforementioned nonexistent baffles. During the course of a morning's hunt, the down would migrate, well, down, thinning the insulation around Larry's shoulders and adding more than he needed around his gut. So when he finally stood up, rail-thin Larry looked like John Goodman with a pinhead. He would then pound and slap at his midsection as he shrugged some feathers back up onto his shoulders.

"Cold?" I'd venture.

"No," he'd say, as if it were a really dumb question. "I've got goose down in here."

"Oh," I'd say. "Right." And we'd hunker back down, looking for geese out past Larry's cardboard silhouette decoys, the ones he'd made tweleve years before. Corrugated box material, actually, according to the story I've heard now just exactly as many times as I've been hunting over them.

"Jeez," he'd muse from the blind. "I never expected those things to last this long. Did I ever tell you the story…"

"Yes."

"…of why I made them? Yeah. First time I came down here to hunt geese, I got an invite from Pete and I didn't have time to make some good ones. You know, plywood. So I had these old moving cartons, and I made a template, cut a couple dozen, painted them and stapled 'em to garden stakes. It took no time, and I'd have been happy to use them just that once. But when they dried out they were fine. Took 'em the next time, and they were still OK. I don't know, the salt water or something, maybe. Anyway, here they are."

We'd both look at them.

"Kind of amazing, you know?" he'd say. One year, about seven or eight into the life of those silhouettes, Larry and I went to Alaska to hunt waterfowl with our mutual friend, John, who lived (still does) in Fairbanks. Larry brought the cardboard geese and John's face positively lit up when he saw them coming around on the baggage-claim carousel, neatly tied together with bleached lobster-pot warp.

"You make new ones for this trip?" he asked Larry.

"No. I just repainted the old ones."

John looked at him and grinned. "That qualifies," he said.

We were going to travel to duck camp in John's twenty-foot freighter canoe — the one he designed and built himself. I knew the silhouettes would get reverent packing by John.

"What'd *you* bring?" he asked me. He knew I didn't make stuff.

"Larry," I answered.

He nodded. "That too," he said.

Among the things that had Larry fired up about the Alaska trip — his first — was the prospect of getting some new duck carcasses. He's a fine carver and likes to work from good reference, so over the years he's collected and preserved the fully-feathered skins of every waterfowl species he could get his hands on. Some of them he's then gone on to turn into lifelike mounts, doing as good a job as any working taxidermist I know, but most of them have remained salted and dried skins, with beak, feet and wings in place, that Larry uses primarily for color and plumage guides as he paints the decoys he's carved. The carcasses lie on the upper shelves of his workshop like the life's work of a halfhearted natural historian. But Larry is anything but disinterested, and his heart is always at full pump.

A couple years before we made the Alaska trip, Larry and I were in a blind on a Massachusetts marsh with our friend Reed and Reed's young Labrador retriever. The dog was, I think, two — strong, fast, and really ready to go.

All we expected that day were black ducks, with the faint chance of a mallard or a late-southing greenwing teal. We had one or two already when a pair came straight at us, cupping their wings fairly far out.

When they were over the narrow, almost-empty salt creek in front of us, we stood and they flared.

They were the first pintails I'd ever seen over Massachusetts salt water.

"Pintails!" shouted Larry. *Bang! Ba-Bang! Bang!* And down came the drake falling hard into the grass across the mud of the creek. Reed's dog was out of the blind like the shots that galvanized him.

Larry was horrified: "Call that dog back!" he yelled.

Reed was horrified: "What?"

Larry was out of the blind and running. "He'll ruin the bird!" he exclaimed. "Hey!" he shouted, running after the dog. "Whoa! Sit! Stop! Come back!"

The dog hit the silty mud of the creek and started slopping across. Larry hit the mud two strides behind him, and the dog stopped when he heard it. You could see *What the hell is this?* written all over his retriever face. Larry lurched through the knee-deep muck toward the dog, and then went right past him. The dog looked at Reed, who had no advice to offer, and back at Larry, who by now was clambering up onto the harder ground of the marsh top. That did it. The race was on.

Larry turned and saw the dog

coming. Panic was in his eyes. “Where’s the bird?” he shouted to us.

“Over there,” Reed and I yelled together, both pointing. Larry bolted in that direction, showing good speed for an older guy in waders.

“First time I ever gave hand signals to a guy,” said Reed.

“Let’s see if he’ll quarter,” I said. Then loud, to Larry: “Whoa. Over that way!” I waved my arm to the left.

Larry stopped, squinting. “What?” he called.

I waved more, but the dog was nose-down going the other way. In sailboat racing it’s called “covering,” making sure you stay in front of the other boat even if neither of you

is on the most direct tack to the finish line. Larry, a member of no yacht club, did it instinctively, cutting back in front of the dog and waving his arms as distraction. He spotted the bird with his eyes just as the dog caught the hot, near scent. They both went for it like NFL linemen after a goal-line fumble.

Larry — was there any doubt? — came up with the pintail. He stood and held it up, out at arm’s length, as the dog danced and jumped for it. Carrying it that way he came back to the blind, breathing hard and grinning ear-to-ear.

The bird was beautiful, in full plumage without any pinfeathers, its long tail arcing out over Larry's cradling glove as he smoothed it with his other hand. The dog sat there, panting and sniffing at the bird.

"I never would have guessed this," Larry said. "Would you?"

Reed and I looked at each other. Reed looked at his dog. Then at Larry.

"No," he said finally. "Not really."

Chapter Six

Duxbury

When you live in the city, like I used to, you go duck hunting before work.

It's a decision you can't make until 11:15 the night before — that's when the late weather forecast comes on the tube.

In an augury worthy of Cassandra herself out of the random jumble of isobars, occluded fronts, and radiational cooling comes the word: duck weather. A call to Kenny or Charley or Niles, a quick inventory of gear and clothing, resetting the alarm to what the Marines call "o'-dark-thirty," and into the sack around midnight. It seems exciting at the time.

Not quite so at four the next morning. In the city you can't tell about the weather unless it's really blowy or wet, and if the stuff isn't rattling off the windows, you'll try to talk yourself into staying between the sheets. But you get up anyway, fry three eggs because you once read something about protein and blood sugar, and while you're eating and putting coffee in the Thermos you peer out at the city street five floors down.

Through the frozen branches of the stunted city-trees are the cars and the hydrants, street lights steady white and the others blinking yellow at one moving car — a cab, empty. The wind, shifting around buildings, throws water from the fire escape against the window. You're going duck hunting.

In the car it's cold, and the heater won't work until you get past the stoplights and onto the expressway. There you'll see a few other cars, men going somewhere at 4:30 in the morning, and the all-night gas station on East Berkeley Street, attentively well-lit on the edge of the ghetto.

You stopped there once two seasons ago, but the attendant was worried by your camouflage clothing and gun case on the back seat. While the pump was running you could see him on the phone, and he left it off the hook when he came back out to take your money. You didn't want to have to explain it to a third-shift cop in that part of town, so you've stayed away since.

The expressway leads out of the city, past the warehouses and gas-storage tanks, past the harbor and the apartment complexes, and soon you're running south, alone, and the road lit only by your headlights. It's a half-hour to the landing nearest the marsh, about the time you need to shed your city-guard and begin to put on the other one, the one you'll need this morning.

Niles will be there at the ramp, already in his waders and rigging the boat; false dawn will be in the east as you crank the rig down to the water, the skim ice breaking crisply against the transom and a couple of decoys thumping hollow as they roll out of the bag and under the thwart. The sculling oar is cold and sandy, wet in your hands as you hold the bow pointed toward the unseen marsh while Niles tries to start the little outboard.

Out in the marsh it's blowing, and you're both wet by the time you get to the bend in the tidal creek. Throw out the decoy bags and gear, step out into the muck, and Niles motors the boat up the creek, out of sight.

One at a time in the cold water you set the decoys, while the soft mud underneath sucks the waders off your feet. It would be easier to stand on the hard ground and toss the blocks out, but too often they land upside down and you have to go out waist-deep to get them. So you do it slowly, leaning out of the mud with each step, ducks upwind to the left, geese downwind and further out in the channel. Always the chance for a goose; rarely the gliding, quick-honking reality of the big birds coming in. Maybe this morning.

Niles is back and has set the blind — burlap, broom handles, grass, two old Canada Dry cases to sit on — facing east into the lightening sky. You get in, shift uncomfortably on the seat, find the magnums. Any time now.

Sea gulls in the air are suspect; sometimes they turn into ducks if you look away. So you don't. Except when the shorebirds dip in over the decoys, in tight formation, turn, flash and gone.

Any time now.

There they are, coming in low over the barrier beach, flaring up past the dunes, turning in toward the tidal creek. Three of them. Black ducks.

Head down, hands over your knees, gun muzzle below the burlap. Listen for the wing-whistle, don't look up; they'll pass overhead for sure if they' re coming in. The mud between your feet is black and wader-printed, oozing. There's an old shell casing in the corner of the blind; that patch on your ankle is beginning to peel, not surprising since it's been four years since you ripped it on Kenny's chicken-wire blind...

Right overhead now, then past, all three turning back. From the right, into the wind, set wings. Just outside the decoys, ten feet off the water. Now.

One is close in, flares away. Track, track... shoot. The shotgun noise is always so different on the marsh, metallic-sounding and muted, sucked away by the wind and the distance.

One bird goes down,

hard. The other two melt downwind, low and hard, then rise steeply, and are gone. Niles is out of the blind, quickly going to the boat to get the bird, now drifting feet up toward the far bank.

You stand and watch, hands in your pockets against the cold. Your toes are numb, ears and nose faintly burning. Spirit quiet, feeling the distance.

Away across the sere grasses and meandering creeks is hard ground, trees and boarded-up summer cottages, the road. The car. The time.

You pull the wrist band of your duck coat up and look at your watch. The hands are there, pointing, not registering. Yes, you'll be very late getting to work. In the city.

A hard shiver gets under your coat, between your shoulder blades and into the back of your throat. The marsh is so wide, mudwet and windy, and there are only birds in it.

Niles reaches the black duck, and picks it up. He holds it up for a second, then sits and turns the boat back up the creek.

And away over the marsh, high up and moving inland, are the geese, wavy line of fifty. Very faintly, and from long, long ago, they call, the cries coming to you sporadically, on the lip of the wind.

Not today, you say. Not today.

Chapter Seven

Minto

It's so hard to keep all the promises you make, especially the ones that arise in the heat of enthusiasm. One that I did keep, however, was the one I made to Casey that opening day in the Ipswich fog. Becky and I did take him to Alaska.

We went to the Minto Flats, northwest of Fairbanks and up toward the Yukon River, a vast region of meandering rivers, tundra and miles-wide marshes from which much of the Pacific Flyway gets its annual cascade of waterfowl. The year we went with Casey, the daily limit was ten birds per person, any species, either sex. In the week we hunted it, we took mallards, pintails, gadwall, goldeneyes, lesser Canadas, shovelers, bluebills, green- and blue-winged teal, and even a canvasback, legally, the only one I've ever shot. Or ever will, I think.

John Hewitt and Ron Rau took us there;

both had lived for the previous decade in and (in Rau's case) around Fairbanks and had gone with tents and canoes to Minto during opening week of the duck season every year. Not many can call that wild and rarely-visited a place their home hunting ground, but they did then. And John, as far as I know, still does.

To get there, we drove in two trucks part way up the pipeline haul road and then took a left, staying on the Elliot, a road only an Alaskan would call a highway, til we found the eleven-mile spur road that ended our 120-mile drive at the tiny Tanana Athabascan village of Minto, on the northern edge of the Flats themselves. From a twenty-foot bluff at the edge of town, just above the place where we would put in our two freighter canoes, we stopped and looked out across the flats. For as far as you could see, toward a level horizon that had more in common with the ocean than with anything this far inland, there was fresh water and low grass, a scattered few islands of yellow birch, all in varying shades of late green and autumn yellow, silver crinklings of shallow potholes and darker ribbons of meandering creeks. Flying ducks were constantly visible, moving across the expanse at every distance, in singles, pairs, and small groups. A bald eagle soared low to the southeast, hunting alone. It was hard to believe that we were here. But we were, it was late in the day, and there remained a long, wet, cold, motorized canoe ride to the campsite where we would pitch our tents, one big one to sleep in and another to keep our duffel dry and out of the way.

It was dark by the time we got that done, and well past eleven by the time we had fed ourselves and the two dogs (John had his golden retriever Jessie along too), set up the gear and guns for the morning, decided who was going to hunt with who and loaded the two canoes accordingly, and finally gone to bed, crawling into our sleeping bags in John's big tent. The dogs slept in there with us. I fell asleep wondering if there were bears.

In the morning — or more accurately well before morning was as much as a proposal in the eastern sky — we got up and made breakfast over an open fire. A big breakfast of eggs, bacon, oatmeal, rolls, juice, coffee. We weren't planning on coming back to camp before lunchtime, six or eight hours away. Thinking about that as I finished a metal cup of strong coffee, I went to one of the cache bags before somebody ran it up a tree and grabbed a pocketful of candy bars. And another for Becky.

"I already got mine," she said as I tried to give them to her. "Thanks."

"Thanks yourself," I answered. "For getting me some when you did."

"Every man for himself," she shrugged.

"I'll remember that when the first birds come into the decoys."

"You better," she said, still deadpan. "If you want to get one."

"Hmmm," said John as he got up to douse the cookfire, trying to keep a straight face. "This could get interesting. Maybe you two shouldn't hunt together right away, least not til you get the edge knocked off. A man wouldn't want to break off a hunt the first day, just to make a long run back to town."

"Long run for what, Bobby Lee?" asked Ron, coming up from the river where he'd been loading a canoe. He and John called each other Bobby Lee and Hiram respectively, names taken from a piece of Flannery O'Connor fiction the edges of which they both sometimes inhabited in their real lives. Or so they liked to claim. Especially Rau. And he was, I thought then and haven't changed my mind since, probably right.

"Oh, I don't know, Hiram," answered John. "Stitches. Splints. Die-vorce lawyers."

"Oh," said Ron. "Well I already did all those, Bobby Lee. Let's go duck huntin'."

"Sounds like a plan," said John as he poured a number 10 can of cold river water on the fire, killing the flames and sending a steaming shower of embers and thick smoke billowing up into the darkened birch trees that surrounded the campsite. When the last remnants of the fire were tamped out, we all shuffled off in our waders and camouflage parkas, down toward the canoes with the two dogs bouncing beside us in the marsh grass. Casey came up beside me as we did, wagging and panting happily under the glittering pre-dawn stars of a cloudless sky. We were in Alaska, and we were going duck hunting.

We set up in two blinds about a quarter mile away from each other, Becky's and mine on one of the tiny yellow-birch islands and Ron and John beside an open-water pothole, hiding behind a grass-covered esker that they called "The Dike." Almost every feature of the places we would hunt that week had a name, a private one that John and Ron had given it over the years they had hunted there. Becky and I were this morning on "Clyde's Island," a name found only on John's carefully-annotated topo maps of the Flats, and in his even more thoroughly annotated mind. I believe that he still remembers every shot he's ever taken there, perhaps every bird that ever came in — or didn't come in — to the decoys he set out there. Definitely every retrieve that Jessie, and the dogs that have followed her, have made there. Calling someone's home hunting ground "sacred" is borderline banal in almost every case, but for John Hewitt the Minto Flats are underserved by the term. An invited guest occupies one of its gunning sites the way a thoughtful visitor enters Carnegie Hall or Lambeau Field: important things have happened here, and the seat you take has been held before.

The first birds that came in were a pair of shovelers, right at first light, unhesitant and looking like mallards in the purple gloom. It was too soon to shoot but I said it anyway.

"Don't shoot. They're Daffys."

"I know."

Shovelers are edible but far from good, and using up part of your bag limit on one is a lost opportunity to take home a mallard or a pintail. In Minto, those two were all that John and Ron wanted to shoot, taking any other species only by accident or as a late-in-the-day second choice, and then only from a time-honored backup list of gadwall, teal, whistlers, and bluebills. At the very bottom of the list was the lowly shoveler. Bringing one back to camp in your daily bag was a sure source of derision and a one-way ticket to doing the dishes after that night's meal, the one during which you would get to eat the shoveler while the others dined elegantly on spit-roasted greenheads and pintails.

The two shovelers landed and immediately began to feed among the dozen Carry-Lite decoys. Sitting between Becky and me, Casey began to quiver as he watched them.

"I know," I said quietly, stroking his back. "I know." The dog's eyes shifted upward as I spoke to him, and I turned to look.

Another pair was coming in from straight out. Not shovelers. As I watched, trying to make them out, something flashed in from my right: ducks, already wing-set, feet down. Mallards, I realized, just as a group of six came in hard from the left, where the shovelers had come from. Gadwalls, I thought. It was still too dark to tell.

"Damn," I whispered.

"How much longer?" hissed Becky.

"Let's wait till we hear them shoot," I answered.

It wasn't that dark: I could see her turn and look at me like I was nuts. "Okay," I relented. "Two minutes." She looked at her watch. According to mine we were already legal, but I really didn't want to start the shooting, not here in John's best place, the first morning of the year's best week.

A minute and a half later, a big group came in fast, buzzed the feeding birds already on the water, lifted like blown leaves in a sudden gust, turned and started back in. They were at least a dozen, closer to twenty, erratically coming right at us and it was now light enough to make them out.

"Bluewings!" I said, "We want them."

We stood up just as they set their wings and

we fired simultaneously as they flared, scattering in all directions, beating for altitude. Two of them came down as the rest of the ducks erupted from the shallow pothole, frothing the water and leaving in as many directions as had the escaping teal. Casey bolted, launching himself ten feet out onto the water with his first bound, splashing through the eighteen-inch depth and right into soft bottom with all fours, barely missing a stride as he bound up and continued on, leapfrogging in a loud, showering straight line toward the first of the two downed teal lying on either side of the erratically bobbing set of decoys in the disturbed water left behind by all the departing ducks. There had been two or three times as many on the water as I had seen coming in. Where had they come from?

Bang! Bang! Ba-bang-bang! Bang! From behind us and to my right, John and Ron both shot pumps. In a place like this the third shot — which neither Becky nor I had in her Model 21 and my battered old Spanish-made double that John called "El Diablo" — would come into play more often than it wouldn't. Odds were that the other two now had six birds in the bag. John's as good an amateur shot as I know and Ron, though streakier, could hold his own with him.

Casey brought in the first bluewing and went back for the other, quartering and hunting hard. Back on our home marsh in Massachusetts, I'd worked in the off seasons with him on marking doubles, using retrieving dummies, but he rarely got a chance to work a pair for real, in a hunting situation; our daily limit on black ducks was down to two by then, and we rarely took them both even when we could. While he rooted around out there in the pothole, Becky and I looked carefully at the teal, the first either of us had held. Five years later we'd be together in a mangrove swamp in the Yucatan, poled in by a Mayan guide who spoke no English but uttered fluent bluewing using just his hands and mouth, and we'd shoot them in good numbers, but here in Alaska this was the first one. If we'd been more European I think we might have poured something from a silver flask and toasted the kill, even at that hour. But we weren't, and we didn't. Instead we laid it out carefully on the ground between us, spreading a wing and admiring the powder-blue sheen of the speculum feathers. The natural world might have sustained itself just as effectively had it evolved without adding random color as it grew, but we'd be living on a poorer planet if it had.

The day's shooting only got better after that. Better in the sense that the birds didn't come in so often or in groups that large. Instead they appeared across ten- to thirty-minute intervals, in pairs and threesomes, and only about half of those that did were mallards and pintails. That's pretty close to a recipe for stretching out a morning's duck hunting without flagging your attention or lulling you back toward the night's sleep you didn't get. Sometime near mid-day, when almost an hour had passed with no birds moving, I heard John's twenty-horse outboard start up over near their blind and ten minutes later he and Ron appeared in the freighter canoe, coming toward us in the winding channel that connected that morning's two shooting spots.

That would be the pattern for the next five days: the morning shoot over decoys, back to camp for lunch, out again in the afternoon, trying something different each time. We'd surround a pothole or spread out along The Dike, looking for mid-afternoon pass shots; some of us would try sneak-shooting along brushy creeks or in a canoe down the main branch of the river; decoys would be moved to different sloughs. We always set out goose silhouettes in the drier grass above the floodline and on the third day Becky got one with a long, high passing shot on a lesser Canada that Rau, crouching beside her, had decided not to try, thinking it was out of range. It wasn't, as we all had a long time to ponder and wonder at, watching it fall and fall and continue to fall, finally landing with a heavy *thud!* on the marsh top between the four of us. It was the highlight film of the trip and we played it back over and over again jointly around cookfires and while waiting for birds to fly and privately, each of us alone in a sleeping bag late at night in our enclosed tent of good friends and tired dogs, sometimes to praise Becky and others times to razz Rau, who may still wake up occasionally in the dark, wherever he is these days, wanting to transport himself back to that one moment in his time, just for a split second, the one in which he chose not to lift his gun toward the that high-flying Canada goose, the only one that any of us would get on that trip to the Minto Flats, in Alaska, in the perfect glory of late September, when we were all just exactly where we wanted to be.

Chapter Eight

South of the Border

When I first woke up, I had no idea where I was. It was dark and I was alone in a metal-frame bunk that I had never slept in before. Other people were sleeping nearby and there was a warm, pre-dawn breeze coming through a large, floor-to-ceiling screen next to the bed. In the distance a coyote yipped, joined by another, then more, the sounds melding and rising hysterically into a full-fledged chase, somewhere out there in the Tamaulipan dark.

Tamaulipan. Tamaulipan. Right. Okay. I was in Mexico. On a dove shoot. Invited here with Chet Reneson and eight other guys for a long weekend at the south-of-the-border hunting lodge owned by a Houstonian who had flown us all down to McAllen where we had crossed over the Rio Grande in Chevy

Suburbans and had driven a half-day to the lodge where we had unpacked our guns and clothing, had dinner, played cards, drunk a few pitchers of margaritas and fallen into our bunks on this second-story, three-sided, screened-in sleeping porch where I had just awakened. Somewhere downstairs a light came on and up here on the porch some of the others stirred, grogging toward wakefulness.

"Hear them coyotes?" said someone in a Texas drawl. You know you're on a certain kind of hunting trip when the first thing you hear on the first morning of the first day, before you've even had a cup of coffee, is the sound of an otherwise educated and well-employed man dumbing himself down to sub-Gomer level in order to converse with the other educated and well-employed men on the trip. But since I took it up while I was in the Navy in Virginia I've always enjoyed dove shooting, something I don't get to do very often from up here in New England, so when Chet arranged the invitation for us both I went happily along. I'd never been on an out-of-the-country dove shoot and had always wanted to try one out.

But even though I knew pretty much what to expect when I got there — this private lodge was the only one on the 100,000-acre corporate farm owned by a family that lived in Mexico City — I wasn't really prepared for the reality of it. I don't think I'd ever shot more than eight or ten birds on a single day in my life, and those few times had been on twelve-bird-limit dove shoots in Virginia.

So when the ten of us in Mexico came back to the Texan's lodge after the first morning's shoot with a pickup truck's bed filled with whitewings, I was pretty much done with it even though we had two more days of shooting ahead of us. It didn't matter that people were on hand to pluck every bird, that not one was wasted; that we ate them with gluttonous abandon while we were there and gave the rest to the farmworkers' grateful families; that we didn't inflict a measurable fraction of a piece of a smidgen on the tens of thousands of birds we saw in just that small pocket of Mexico; or that every future kernel of corn that didn't go into the mouth of one of those doves that we did shoot was a kernel that would go into a tortilla that a hungry local kid could wrap his hands around the following winter. Well, okay, I take that back; it did matter. Some. But not enough. At least not for me. I'm not sure where between the anticipation and challenge of the morning's first incoming dove and the reality of the last one tossed into the pickup truck that the day's take became excessive, but somewhere it did. Somewhere along the way — and I don't think it was any too close to the end — the gradual accumulation, the just-one-more-bird accretion that measures every bird hunt everywhere, became in this case an unseemly heap. But how were we to know exactly when? With which individual bird should someone have said, "That's it. One more and it'll be too many." We couldn't say because there wasn't one, any more than it was that one straw that broke the camel. It was the guy who kcpt adding to the load, wasn't it? It was the guy who kept reloading his gun, wasn't it? And wasn't that guy me?

When we got back to the lodge we all ate a big lunch and then almost everyone there settled back into the cooling shade of the sleeping porch for a two-hour siesta. Everyone but Chet and me.

"I don't know about these other guys," said Chet, "but I came down here to hunt, not sleep. I can do that at home."

"You don't want more doves, do you?" I asked.

"Not like that I don't," he dismissed. "Didn't you see that little slough on the driveway where we came in?"

"Yeah, I did." Lying a five-minute walk from the lodge was a ten or twenty-acre lowland, wet and swampy, green with shoulder-high grass and varieties of brushy vegetation that I couldn't name.

"Well, Péron says a few doves come in there in the afternoon for water. He says you can hunker down and shoot them like you're duck hunting."

"Ah, I don't know, Chet. I'm kinda shot out on doves."

"Yeah? What would you rather do, sleep in the middle of the day? I'm not that old and you sure as hell aren't." Chet's always had as much energy as a bird dog. Maybe more; my dogs do sleep in the middle of the day. But none of them would have said no here.

"Okay," I said. "Let's do it."

We hadn't brought waders or hippers, but we both had high leather boots for snakebite prevention and we wore those down into the little wetland. It was 2:30 in the afternoon and hot, but we found some shade under a sort of willow tree beside an open bit of standing water that was maybe three inches deep and twenty yards in diameter. Separating by ten yards, we hunkered down out of sight and waited.

Nothing happened. We waited for half an hour. Nothing happened. I began sliding toward a siesta in spite of myself.

A bird whizzed by, behind us.

"Get down!" hissed Chet, sounding more urgent than he should have, given the number of doves we'd already seen that day. I was already down, but I swiveled, scanning.

A small flight of birds came in fast, left to right and out of the corner of my eye I saw Chet coming up, gun pointing, just as I brought my own up and began tracking the six — green-winged teal!

I stopped swinging in surprise. Chet didn't: *Bang! Bang!* from my left where he was. I recovered, tracked a bird as they veered and scattered, fired. It twisted away, still flying. I fired again and down it came, tumbling into the tall grass across from us. Quickly I turned back, looking for another bird. We were shooting the lodge's house guns — Remington 870s with the plugs removed. I had three shots left, but the remaining birds were already gone.

"Which way did they go?" I called to Chet.

"What do you mean 'they'?" he said. "You mean 'it'."

"How many did you get?" I asked.

"Four."

He had. While I fumbled and tracked my one bird, he had knocked down four, smoothly popping the pump gun like it was an automatic. I should have known, of course. In his and Penny's house in Connecticut, on a rack across from the wood stove, is a line of well-worn and longtime-owned Model 12s in all gauges and barrel lengths; the classic Winchester is the only gun he shoots when he has the choice.

It took us a few minutes to locate all the teal, but we did, and then we carried them back to the lodge where the siesta-takers had rallied at the sound of our shooting.

"Well hail now," said one. "Ah dint know this thang was a die-em duck hunt or I'd a come along with y'all."

Chet grinned and so did I. We looked at each other and then at the lawyers, insurance brokers and investment bankers turned weekend good ol' boys who stood around us, grinning back. But we dint say a die-em thang. Just warn't no pint in it. No pint a tall.

Chapter Nine

Down East

You always see them in the spring and summer, usually in pairs but often enough in ragged strings above the lakes and bogs of fishing time.

The summer geese and ducks are an increment, an expected decoration for the long days and cool twilights of the north country in full bloom. You'll be paddling around a bend at the inlet to Musquadabook Lake, easing into the flat water and pickerel grass and reaching for your rigged fly rod, when three mergansers will come zipping by, ten feet off the water and cruising.

Or maybe you'll be sitting at the morning fire, a high overcast softening the light as the woodsmoke slips straight up and someone else is doing the breakfast clean-up. You've just finished your second cup of coffee and as you start to get up to help you see them. Black ducks, you figure, but maybe mallards… seven, no, eight of them across the lake and above the spruces, heading south.

Heading south.

But no, you say, it's just chance. They're not leaving yet. Not in August.

Sure. Don't worry. It's still fishing.

Yeah, right. Fishing.

But…

But what?

But the teal have already left.

The teal have… No, I saw some yesterday. Greenwings.

Oh, some are still here. They haven't all left.

Yeah.

. . .

What?

Seen any bluewings?

This year, up on the lake in August, the fishing really is excellent. A wet year has kept the streams high and the water temperature down; trout are active in the streams and bass are still on top, looking for poppers. You don't have to fight the mosquitos at twilight just to get in a little surface action, and today is a bonus: clouds to keep the sun off the water.

So it's the long paddle to the rocks and bars at the end of the lake, a day trip that you don't make every year, waiting for a year like this and a day to match so that the time spent in transit down there and back to camp will pay off. You don't even want to think about a headwind.

And there is none now, none likely later. At the end of the lake, an hour after breakfast, you find that the fish have moved away from the rocks and are moving in the weeds and pads of shallow water.

So you move in with them.

And watch in gaping stupor as thirty Canada geese get up honking a hundred yards in front of the canoe. It takes them a full two minutes to get out of sight over Firetower Hill to the west.

Did you see that?

Did I see it?

Geese. There are geese up here.

Yeah, I know.

Well…

Well, they weren't heading south.

Not yet, you mean.

Look…

Okay, okay.

A mid-morning lull in the fishing, still in the shallows, down lake. You put down the fly rod and reach for the old ammo can to get at the binoculars.

Looking for more geese?

No. Just looking.

Mmmmm…

I am. Just looking.

Right.

Blue heron over there…

You know you…

…fishing.

…can…

What? What now?

All I was saying was that you can use that ammo can for ammo, you know.

I know. I do. At home on the duck hunts. You know that.

Yeah.

And a bit later, after the heron moves off and all the other grey possibilities are resolved into the stumps and hillocks of reality, you put down the binoculars, reach again for the fly rod.

Some people do it, you know.

Do what?

Hunt this country.

Of course they do.

For ducks.

Yeah.

And geese.

I know. But they're locals.

You could do it, you know.

I know.

You could do it just like you are now. A couple of canoes. Bring the wall tent and the dog.

Decoys. Set up for three or four days and work the marshy edges...

I do know.

Sure you do.

I do. I've always thought about it. It's been in my mind since Kenny first came up here and saw the marshes and the birds. I think about it a lot on the long drive up and back every year. It's a good thing. I'll do it.

This year?

I don't know.

. . .

Well, I don't. It's tough getting the time.

. . .

It *is*. And it's no sure thing, you know. I don't know when the birds pack up out of here. I don't know when the lakes ice up.

. . .

Well, it's true.

. . .

What?

How much younger are you getting?

Chapter Ten

Thanksgiving

On Thanksgiving we'll start the day earlier than most of the others. The night before we'll have set the alarm for an hour before sunrise, but one of us will awaken before it goes off, rising to the certain tick of a circadian clock that always goes duck hunting on Thanksgiving morning.

In the bedroom we'll put on turtlenecks and long underwear, wool shirts and socks, and then we'll pad quietly down to the basement, stopping to knock gently on the doors of the hunters, and taking care not to waken the rest.

We'll stop in the kitchen to put fire under the coffee pot, boil eggs, and cook toast. It's a quick and light breakfast, but it's going to be cold out there and we'll all need the calories burning inside.

In the basement the light will be white and stark from the naked bulbs and there will be a momentary clutter of rubber and canvas, graceless torsos stumbling into awkward gear until the action sorts itself into a quieter hierarchy of those ready and those still dressing. Against the far wall the guns are neatly lined up, dark wood and worn blue, gleaming parallel in the basement light. Somebody opens a Thermos, pours coffee, passes it around.

"Quarter to six. Let's go." It's the Thanksgiving shoot.

Outside the cold is a wall; wind comes hard from the north, and there are no stars. The canoes are there, tied to the old dock and resting on the marsh grass; decoys are stacked in each, paddles, and there is solid ice that breaks crinkly when someone lifts a paddle.

Each of us knows where to go. The blinds have been selected, tested and gunned during seasons past, other Thanksgivings gone by now, and the night before we will have drawn lots for them. Horse-trading will have followed, always, a kitchen clean-up assignment swapped for a spot in the pit at Two Bird Cove, or a seat in the board blind where French's Creek widens at the second big bend.

It won't really matter, though. The birds will ride the wind and play the tide, and the shooting will come as it may. Maybe it won't come at all, like the year the warm front came through on the Tuesday before, and the inland ponds melted, and the birds went inland, and nobody even saw a bird all morning, and Uncle Patrick got so frustrated he stood up and threw his new Ithaca into the water in front of the blind, and he had to go back out at low tide and drag it up out of the mud.

Or maybe it will be like the year the squall line came in off the ocean, pushing squadrons of black ducks, Canada geese, whistlers, and even the brant into the marsh, and after some of us had gotten limits we stayed and watched the action at the other blinds, cheering out loud for good dog work and hooting derision at emptied-gun misses, and Uncle Stephen had been just so damned pleased with the whole business he decided to stay in his hunting clothes all day and tried to come to Thanksgiving dinner in his waders.

Every year it's something to remember. And now it's this year, canoes slipping down the tide in the early cold of Thanksgiving morning, a lean wind coming out of the north, and dawn just a promise behind the clouded eastern sky.

Out in the marsh, we'll spread out; there will be six, maybe seven of us, a dozen decoys to put out in front of the three blinds, a few silhouettes stuck in the marsh upwind, and then we'll be ready.

Shooting light will come very slowly, and before we can see at all, there will be whistling beats in the wind above us, an early pair splashing long into the set in front of Sam and Becky. Sam will be excited, will want to jump up and take an early shot, but Becky will know better. Too dark yet, she'll say. Let them be natural decoys. And Sam will fidget, head swiveling in the growing light, wishing in the birds. They'll come.

They'll come in pairs and three's all morning long, coming low over the dunes, flaring up to survey the marsh and then banking in wide, gliding turns over one of the sets, swinging fast twenty feet in the air to turn abruptly with braking wings, feet out and stopping in midair. *Bang!*

They will be black ducks, mostly, and the odd bufflehead. The teal will have moved on, and it will be too early for geese, but it will be just fine with us. The black duck is right for the Thanksgiving shoot, complementary to a turkey and carefully plucked for Saturday's dinner, a somewhat rowdier affair than the quiet formality of the Thanksgiving meal itself. A duck for everyone is the goal this morning.

And by ten, we'll have succeeded or failed. Plenty of birds will have been over the decoys, and we'll have had the shots. Doug will have made a long double, his first, and won't be feeling the cold at all. Caroline might have gotten a bird, might not; sometimes we suspect she misses on purpose, but she's taken them cleanly before, and she's been hunting the longest of the four.

Back at the house, the others will have risen, made breakfast, and the hunters will gather in the kitchen over coffee and hot chocolate, milling about and already re-telling the funny part, stalling over another piece of toast until plucking time. Then it will be showers, better dress, indoor manners, the holiday meal. The Thanksgiving shoot will have passed.

The Thanksgiving shoot. The one that, twenty-three years ago, I was certain would happen, sometime in what was then the future. I had been sitting on the back porch, plucking a pair of black ducks and intent on what I was doing, when I looked up to see Hope, still in her pajamas with the feet on them, standing there. I plucked a wing feather, dark on the back, white underneath, and handed it to her. She took it, smiling past the thumb in her mouth, and without saying a word went back into the house.

She didn't say a thing about it all day, but that night when we tucked her into bed, I turned just as I switched off the light. And there on her shelf among her treasures and teddy bears, lying quietly beside Bunny Rabbit and her extra special crayons, was a wing feather from a black duck, catching the last flicker of room light on an iridescent blue speculum, and flashing to me a Thanksgiving promise of all that lay ahead.

But, as Salvador Dali once said, so little of what is possible actually happens. Where the rest goes — all those things that don't

happen — is, of course, unanswerable even by those who claim it isn't. At least not completely. In the case of my feather-foreshadowed Thanksgiving shoot, the one I just described, it only grew as far as the hunting lives of my family allowed it to. And like any extended set of relatives at the turn of this millennium, most of the people in it are non-hunters. Of my parents' four sons I'm the only regular hunter, and neither Becky's brother nor her sister are shooters. Of Becky's and my children, three of them want to hunt and two don't really care about it. I don't know how this fits into the national averages, but I suspect it's not far off the mark for most gunners of my generation.

But the fact that most of my family doesn't hunt is a misleading measure of how much they like to eat the results brought back by those of us who do. Game dinners are enjoyed by all, and Thanksgiving in our household has always had a large hunting component to it, with varying mixes of waterfowling, upland gunning, and deer hunting taking up much of the daylight in that annual four-day gathering. A few years ago — more than a few now, as I do the arithmetic — my youngest brother Stephen moved up here to New Hampshire from Bronxville, New York, relocating with his wife and two daughters to a house with a few acres and a barn not too far from us; we share Thanksgiving dinner every year, alternating between his place and mine, and usually adding varying numbers of cousins, in-laws, grandparents, house guests and, of course, dogs. The regular number on dogs is, I think, five. Stephen doesn't hunt and never has, but he's always ready to dive into a venison chop or mallard breast, whenever either or both are on the menu, and every time he does I catch this fleeting glimpse of him in my mind, coming to the Thanksgiving table in his chest waders, the ones he only owns in my imagination, the ones he wore on that Thanksgiving hunt that never happened. It's only there for a flicker, but it's truly there, iridescent, shining. And blue.

Chapter Eleven

Integrity

You'll know it when the time comes. There won't be any need for official regulations or the posting of seasons — those things take care of themselves, and they always manage to make things legal for you. The time comes late in the season, every year. It will come again this year.

The week before, it will snow. Hard. For three days. And the northeast wind will push drifts deep into the troughs of the sand dunes along the barrier beach. At the height of the storm the crests of the dunes will shed spumes of sand into the wind, hard-stinging grit that rides in the snow across the channel and onto the marsh.

Then the snow will taper, clouds thin, and the tides will rework their sculpture on the hardened edges of the little creeks. Salt ice cover, a foot thick, will crack and fall in the draining marsh to lie like collapsed tunnels before the rising neap floats them again. Hardened spartina will bend up under the crusting snow, trapped by the weight until group pressure pops a jagged hole and the grasses rise in a mat above the lumpy white.

That night the clouds will blow to sea, and by midnight a hard starry sky will blink down on the subdued marsh. Cold northern night, quiet radiational chiller from the land of tapered meridians, this will be the dark that comes before the time.

False dawn, light without heat, faint hint of the eastern horizon, will find you, shadows

moving on the marsh. Three of you, moving slowly, bent and bundled, stepping cautiously on the grass and snow mat, picking your way along the edge and moving toward the silver twinkle of open water.

At the point of the marsh, where two of the little creeks come together to form a small bay, you will stop, thump wet burlap heavily on the snow crust. The dog, still dry and car-warm, tail-high and excited, will prance and sniff at the decoy bags, then slide down the muck to the sludge ice edge of the creek.

Your partner will drag a line of decoys — cork bodies and pine heads, black, gray and tan, big Canadas — out into the water while you scrape at the snow on the grass, looking for beaten plywood that covers the pit.

The pit. You had found the spot earlier, in the high summer when you were pramming the creek with the little guys, scouting for periwinkles and cherrystones, and you had come back in bright September with your partner to dig the pit. Four feet down, three feet back, seven wide, lined with plywood; bench and shelf, drainage hose, hinged cover and woven grassing. Hours. Hammered thumb. Fishing time given up. The pit.

Now it's here. Ice cracks when you open the lid; inside the mud is frozen hard, like dark brown plaster spilled badly, and the bench is slick and crinkly when you step down on it. Your partner comes back for another string of blocks as you set out the gear in the blind.

Guns out of the canvas, Thermos on the shelf, ammunition in utility boxes — a faint Army memory, bad, gone quickly — and then out of the pit to check the grassing. Snow has covered the storm-blown bare spots. No problem today.

It's coming on real dawn now, and with it the wind, cold beyond gradation, a solid pressure on your chest and pure pain in your face. You can't look into it. Look away.

Your partner is back and the decoys are all out, nineteen pitching geese grouped according to his view of the order of things. Other days you'd need more, silhouettes on sticks out in the flats, but not today, not this late and cold. Today is the time.

In the pit and waiting, you watch the sky. The rising wind brings clouds, gathering gray smothering the early yellow and red of the dawn and cutting off the sun before it can show itself. The cold flows deep, a dark sensation heightened by the shivering dog sitting between you. He'll be okay; underneath he's a furnace burning with focused and retained energy.

So you focus yourself. You know where they will come from, and you have to look into the wind to stay with it. Up in the wind, over the little bay and the breadth of marsh are the sand dunes, shields against the winter sea, low cover for the homing birds. They may be there right now, just outside the barrier, three feet off the water, fanned out and winging steady, coming fast and smooth downwind.

Look for them. Look for them on this last day. Hold fast into the bite of the wind, don't miss any of it. Any of it.

For now it has come down to the simple, the clean, hard end of it. No more ducks, no more shore birds, gulls; no more easy autumn, late sails up in the harbor; no other hunters, blue herons, distant horns or light planes overhead. No more days. One more chance, two tracks on a sure vector. The time. Take all of it. Look hard, don't turn.

There they come.

Over the dunes, half a dozen, rising. Ten, fifteen now, wings steadily beating. Twenty. Thirty, fanned out, coming in off the ocean, winging easily. More coming, fifty now.

There they come… there they come…

Here they come. Half a mile, straight at you. It had to be. You knew it, you knew it. Get your head down.

Hold now in the pit of winter, in the ending cold of it; hold now and watch them as they slide down the wind and spread out, twenty feet off the ground, coming at you. Three hundred yards.

Look at them…

The wings set. A hundred and fifty yards and coasting. Now you must look down and count the seconds. Count them. One… two… three… four… five…

Now. This is the time. This is the time.

Look up.

CHAPTER TWELEVE

TARRED AND FEATHERED

It is March. A winter moon has risen above the line of low hills to the east of the marsh, its cold light catching on a trickle of woodsmoke floating quietly into the night from the kitchen of the old house.

The house is darkened, except for the yellowed glare of a single lightbulb above the kitchen table, and there are two men sitting there. One of the men is quiet, arms folded across his chest as he leans back in his chair. His lips are pursed, eyes squinting slightly as he watches the older man. He seems concerned.

The older man is unshaven; he wears woolen pants with suspenders over a long-sleeved undershirt and his boots are laced halfway, the extra length of lace tucked down against the tongue.

There is a kitchen tumbler partly filled with whiskey and a single piece of melting ice in front of him. He is talking:

I suppose you want to know why I did it. How such a foolproof scheme fell through. Well, don't be embarrassed, they all do. And anyhow, I ain't sorry for what I did, not in the least. But I don't mind telling you that it's still got some sting in it, it does.

Some sting, I don't mind telling you.

The older man reaches for his pipe, which had been lying on the table in front of him. He tamps the tobacco with his thumb and then lights it.

Now, the thing of it is — and you got to understand this, 'cause it's the whole reason for it. I mean, for me it is — but when I was a kid I used to hunt that place. And I mean all the time. Railbirds in September, pushing through that little marsh 'til it looked like a bunch of moose had done bumper cars in there or something. *Goddam*, I remember the time... Well, that's somethin' else. And then the ducks, about mid-October right on through. Blacks, bunches of them little greenie teals, and the mallards. The mallards comin' in offa that piss-ant farm...

'Course it wasn't her farm back then. I mean that's the whole deal. That's where the whole friggin' mess came from, you know. You do know that much, don't you?

Well, the farm, you see, had been there, hangin' on to the marsh ever since old Ike Addison battened down the Indian shutters and told the Squamscotts to go bother someone else. Five *generations* of Addisons had that farm, and every son of 'em knocked out a little more wood and put in a little more corn. So by the time the old man — old man Addison, Chester was his name, he was the last of 'em — by the time *he* come along there must of been three hundred acres of it cleared and planted in those little valleys.

Now I'm not saying that they were going to put Iowa out of business or anything, 'cause that never was what you might call your butter-and-sugar corn, but for a lotta years a lotta folks around here — and a whole *hell* of a lotta cows — put their stock in that Addison corn. It was important to what you might call the local economy. A local economy was the only kind they had back then, you see, because a man had to sort of stand up for himself, you see… Well, that's somethin' else.

Anyway, I guess you must know what happens around here in the fall when you got the biggest stand of cut corn for maybe two hundred miles sittin' right next to the prettiest little salt marsh that three fresh-water brooks ever emptied *in* to. Huh? Well I'll tell you what you got. You got *geese* is what you got. Geese...

The older man leans back in his chair. His eyes lose their focus as he watches the pipe smoke drift past the overhead light to spread against the stained ceiling. The younger man remains quiet.

Anyway, you probly didn't come here for the history of Addison's farm and I'm sorry for bein' windy, but you just gotta understand how come when the kid came up with the idea — it was all the kid's idea, you gotta know that — why it was I went along with it.

Now the kid... Well, I don't know, what's a kid? To me he was, anyway. I don't think he was thirty, nowhere near it; and he was kinda scruffy, if you know what I mean. I mean he had a lotta hair and a beard that was no

accident, and he was wearin' an old fatigue jacket. You know how these kids look... Anyway, the kid came up to the house, very polite, knocking quiet, and he said to me, 'Sir, my name is Sam Douglas and I'd like permission to park my car here so that my dog and I can hunt geese down in that little marsh.'

Well, I get 'em like that — though not usually so polite, you know — two, maybe three times a season. I mean the old lady's got the other side of the road posted so heavy for about two miles that you got to be pretty goddam unfamiliar with the language not to get the message. I guess I'm getting pretty crotchety about it, too, so I stepped out on the porch — not sayin' a word, you know — so I could just sort of point his head at any one of the maybe twenty signs you can see from the porch. I mean she's got 'em all up there — white ones, green ones, some day-glo; big, little, some with a lot of legal stuff, some just pictures of men with those little circles around 'em with a slash through it, you know? Hell, she's even got 'em up there in French 'cause she's afraid some of them loggin' boys she hired a few years back are gonna come back. Christ.

Anyway, I went out there to straighten out the kid, but before I got to it I noticed that the kid's got an old Scout parked there. I'm always lookin' at Scouts, since I can't remember how long it's been since I had anything else, myself, but I've gotta tell you that this one caught my eye because there was an even older Old Town up on to — green, about sixteen feet, real scratchy along the bottom — and inside that Scout was Tar.

The older man stops talking. He sits up straight, eyes wide, taking in air, and then sneezes hard. He takes a wrinkled, gray-yellowed cloth from his pants pocket and wipes his nose back and forth. After the sneeze his left eye is red and watery.

Well, 'course it wasn't really Tar, Tar bein' ten years gone now, but when I looked into that car and saw that black Lab sittin' there, well, I just forgot all about the old lady's friggin' signs.

'Say,' I said to the kid. 'Let's have a look at your dog.'

Now, I'm here to tell you that right there, right at exactly that instant, the whole damn deal was signed, sealed, and delivered. I was in it up to my itchy neck, I want you to know it, and I didn't even know it was *comin'*.

Well, the kid, he just twinkled for a minute. Okay, that sounds a little off, I know, but there's just no other word for it. I mean the kid's eyes just went flashy like all his buttons got pushed at the same time, and without even turnin' his head, mind you, just smilin' at me, he says real soft, real soft:

'Cutter.'

And this black rig comes out the open front window of that Scout. About two leaps and he's sittin' there right beside the kid, tongue out and pantin'. I guess I don't have to tell you that he was right on the kid's left side, at perfect heel.

A muffled flush of falling embers in the woodstove; the older man pulls two pieces of split oak from a neat pile beside the stove, opens the front door with the toe of his boot and pushes the fresh wood into the flickering orange inside.

Okay, I know what folks around here think of my opinions about what's a good dog and what ain't, but you gotta remember that before the old lady over there came into the picture we used to have some pretty fair field trials around here — we even had a couple of live-bird numbers down there in the far field — the one that slopes down to the marsh — and Tar and I never lost one. Hell, we'd still be havin' 'em if the old lady hadn't come down there right after she bought the place…

Now wait a minute. I know what you're thinking about that. Everybody thinks it's all my fault, that it all happened at that field trial, and that's why the place is posted and all, but you gotta remember that I know dogs better'n anyone else. That's why Tar an' me was the best, you see. So when that old lady brings down that piss-ant racing dog of hers I knew there was goin' to be trouble. I just knew that. And when that whippy-ass racer went over and lifted his leg on the live-bird pens... Sweet Jesus, can't you still just see that.

Well, like I always said, with a dog you fight fire with fire and you better get right to it if you're goin' to have any effect at all, so I still don't see why she got so damn excited when I just walked over and peed on her dog. I mean, hell, that dog of hers wasn't any too clean, anyway, and goddam it, it sure stayed away from those bird pens after that, didn't it? Well, didn't it?

The older man reaches for the bottle to pour more whiskey. The cork top rolls off the table, thuds gently on the floor and comes to rest against the woodpile. He stares at it for a minute, then goes on without looking up:

Anyway, the point of it is, I know a good dog when I see one, and this Cutter of the kid's was... well... I don't know how to say it without sounding weird about it, but...

Well, goddamn it, the dog was just amazing, that's all. Just amazing. I mean, the dog's still sitting there at heel — on the porch, remember — and I say to the kid, 'Say, kid, let's see him work a bit.'

Okay, now I know you don't want to hear all about the dog, I know you want to hear about how the old lady got wise to us, but just wait a minute here, because the dog's job down there was… Well, hold up a bit; I'm gettin' ahead of myself there.

The kid, anyway, goes back to the car to get a couple of retrieving dummies — and you *know* that dog never missed a beat at that tight heel the kid had him at — and for the next twenty minutes I'm telling you, I'm ready to fold up and get in the ground 'cause I've seen the best I'm gonna see in this world. *Goddam*, why there was one set of triple blind retrieves where the kid set up a distractin' scent with a fresh mallard wing he had in the Scout, and that Cutter just… Okay, okay, you heard about it, but the point is that after seein' that dog do his number out back, there was no way that I was gonna miss that act in the marsh.

So I asked the kid if he didn't maybe want a beer after that. I mean I was gonna toast that dog with something stronger than water whether the kid was still on Kool-Aid or not, but when I said 'beer' the kid's eyes did that twinkly, flashy item all over again, so I figured he wanted one. Jesus, there's what you call an understatement.

The old man takes a long pull on his whiskey.

Well, I guess everyone in the county knows by now that the kid had probably had a beer or two in his life before I gave him one that afternoon. But I gotta be honest about it, it didn't seem that odd to me when he sucked the first one down real quick. Hell, I didn't know how far he had driven — I still don't know where he came from, or went — but I just figured he was thirsty, was all.

I'll admit now that he wasn't any too shy about askin' for another one right off.

'Now, sir,' he says to me after I get him another cold one. 'About parking my car here while Cutter and I sneak down to your little marsh. Will that be all right?'

Now, you gotta know that after watching that dog work, and then settlin' pretty comfortable into a cold beer, I had completely slipped off about the kid's original intention, and I might have steered him back out to the porch to study the old lady's sign collection, except that — and I still, for the goddam life of me, I still don't know if he knew what he was sayin' — the kid said what you got to know is the magic word:

'Sneak.'

God, I've troubled over it, you don't know how much, ever since, and I just can't figure it. I mean maybe he was thinkin' of jump-shooting or something, or maybe he was just the careful type and didn't want to move any birds out of the marsh when he went in to set up his blind. I mean, maybe the kid really hadn't seen any of the old lady's signs, and maybe it was a word that he used without much thinkin' about it.

I don't know. *Goddam* it, I don't know.

The older man is quiet for a moment, reflecting. Outside the wind is up, pushing hard bits of old snow against the window and rattling stiff oak branches against the house; faintly heard scraping noises coming from the darkened far rooms.

But, you know, there was just enough about the way that he said that word to make me hold back a minute. So I leaned back in my chair, took another pull on the beer, and said, real casual about it, you know:

'What do you want to hunt that little swamp for, kid?'

I was loose about it, didn't even look him in the eye when I said it — stuff like that, you know. Thought I was bein' what you call close to the vest. Smart about it. Christ.

The kid, of course, didn't bat an eye.

'Well,' he says. 'I've been studying it, and from the map, and from what I can see, it looks like a place where geese will go for the night.'

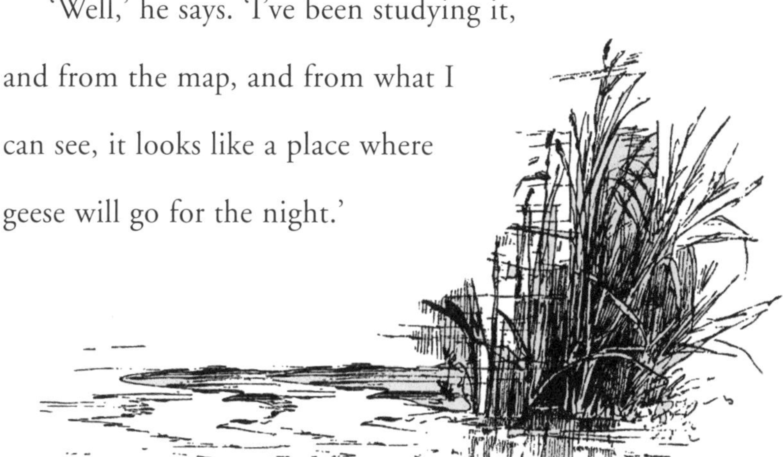

Can you imagine that? For 200 years those big Canadas been comin' in offa that corn, settin' their wings in the evening glow right back there over my barn — and long before that was a barn, I'll tell you, and...

'Well,' I says to the kid. 'Just what do you know about geese?'

'Sir,' he says back. He's lookin' me right in the eye now. 'I live for geese.'

Now maybe you could of thought of something to say to that. I just stared at him. For a minute he stared back, and then he leaned back a little and reached into his jacket pocket.

'Do you mind if I smoke,' he says. And when he pulled out this pipe you could of knocked me down, I'm tellin' you. I mean this pipe-smokin' stuff is sort of reserved for us old farts, you know, and it kinda threw me off when he showed up with that act. 'Course the pipe was a little weird lookin', but you can't expect a kid to get everything just right.

'Hell, no,' I said. 'I'll join you.'

Well, you know how these deals go. Once you got the pipes goin' you can't foul it up with beer, so I got out the sippin' whiskey, which the kid thought was just fine, and once we got the place good an' bluc and had dispensed with the compliments about the good whiskey I was pourin', we got down to talkin' geese.

Funny thing is, though, for a while there was somethin' just off about it, and I couldn't quite get it. I mean, sure the kid wasn't what you might call the right sort of demeanor for this kind of hot stove stuff, but that wasn't it, and it wasn't for a while 'til I got it. It was the kid's tobacco. It was odd smelling stuff, I'll tell you, and it just didn't complement the flavor of good bourbon.

But that's no big deal, right, so as soon as I had put my finger on the story, I figured the hell with it, he'll gain taste with age maybe.

Back to the geese, anyway. And on that topic, I've gotta tell you the kid knew what he was after. Like I said, he was way under thirty, but somewhere along his path the kid had gotten out there after geese a few times. 'Course I'm not sayin' that he had a lot to teach *me*, but for a kid he wasn't too far off the mark on a lotta stuff some pretty good hunters around here still haven't figured out. Like this business on the two-note lonesome call, well, he said he didn't place too much stock in it. Said he preferred...

Yeah, okay, okay. Probly wouldn't do you too much good anyway. And I'm gettin' to the heart of the whole business here, now. Now.

The old man gets up from his chair and walks to the window. Frost etches the panes, and the reflection in the glass is a wobbly dark silhouette, backlit by the single lightbulb. He returns to the table.

Okay, I guess I don't have to go into details of the plan with you, since you sort of know what happened anyway, but you gotta know this: I didn't give the kid hint number one. I mean, for ten years I'd kept my mouth absolutely *shut* about poachin' that marsh, and I wasn't about to open up to that kid, no matter how good his dog was. Or how much whiskey I drank that night, and God knows I had enough.

But the kid, he sure knew the way he wanted to go after the geese in there, and after he got the map spread out right here on this table and started tellin' me about how he figured they'd be in there since just after dark, and would get up in the morning to head up the corn… Well, I gotta admit that I just fell in with the conspiracy. 'Course the thing of it is, the kid was guessin', but I *knew.*

Anyway, now that the jig's up, and the deal is blown forever, there ain't no harm in tellin' how I used to work it. I mean, the old lady always knew I went in there, and it did frost her ass, don't you know it, but she was awful dumb about catching me. All she had to do was take the trouble to study a tide table one time and she'd of had me. Anybody knows that the big tides come once a month, and you can only paddle down Tern Creek on one of them, so when one of the big tides comes high about four-thirty in the morning — and it happens once every gunnin' season, sometimes early, sometimes not until January — that's when I'd slide down there. Once a year, that's all, but there was some shootin' to be had on that day. Goddam.

Well, she never got me, and I'll bet she rousted herself outa the rack 200 mornings over those years, lurkin' about the marsh lookin' for me. Why she…

Okay, back to the kid, I know. Now the thing that I thought was real amazing was that the kid just happened to show up on the night before this year's big tide. Well, that's not exactly right, 'cause this one was at two in the morning, and come December there'd be the one I was going to hunt, since it was going to be at five then, but still.

Yeah, sure. You know how it happened. We got through the bottle and most of my pipe tobacco about one in the mornin', and after we'd talked that marsh to death, and the kid had said maybe ten times that he really thought that if we sneaked down that little creek in his canoe we would be ready for them when they got up, and all the rest… Well, the kid just looks me in the eye and says, 'Let's do it.'

The old man's pipe has been out for some time, and he reaches into his pocket for his tobacco pouch. He quickly refills and lights up, then drains the remaining whiskey in his glass.

Well, let me tell you that you have not lived until you've slipped down Tern Creek in the middle of the goddam night with a snootful of this stuff, a wild-eyed kid with long hair and a fired-up Labrador retriever. Jesus, you should have seen it… Two o'clock in the frigging *morning*. Loaded. A kid I'd never seen before. Jesus.

By the time we get down to the marsh, I'm gonna admit to you that my head was hurtin'. But we get down there — and this'll show you how drunk I musta been — 'cause for the first time I notice that the wind is outa the east. The *east*, for Christ sake. That meant, I guess you probly don't know, that when the birds would get up they were goin' to head right up over the old lady's house. Well, I figured right then that the jig was up, but the kid didn't bat an eye.

'Here,' he says. 'You set up on the little point here, and Tar and I'll paddle over to the east side. Then when the geese get up we'll show ourselves and that'll turn them back over to you.'

'That's all right with me,' I said — I'm tellin' you now that *anything* was all right with me at that point — 'But what about you? I mean the old lady's liable to be right on your ass over there.'

'Don't worry about me,' he says. 'There's two hours 'til shooting light, and that'll give me plenty of time to set up so she'll never find me.'

Now that sounds pretty damn dumb now, but you gotta understand what was goin' on down there. I mean the kid and I had pushed his canoe up against the mud bank — 'course it was a real high tide, so there wasn't much bank, except what I knew was down under that water — and the dog was movin' this way and that, makin' the canoe what you might call unstable. There was no moon, and I figured that a good plan was to get the hell outa that canoe. So when the kid said to get on out and he'd move on across the marsh, that sounded about right to me.

So I grabbed my gun and seat and stepped outa the canoe. Now I'm still tryin' to figure out how such a well-trained dog as that Tar should be so rambunctious in a boat, but damn if he didn't somehow just push that canoe right out from under me and Pop! I'm on my ass in the grass in a foot of water.

Okay, we've all been in the water and who cares, but the bad thing of it was that it wrecked my pipe tobacco — and that marsh wasn't exactly your Saratoga hot springs, neither — so I guess I mighta let the kid know that I wasn't too happy about the turn of events.

Well the kid showed himself to be a pretty

decent sort, had all the right instincts, anyway, 'cause he paddles back over and says, 'Here, try some of mine. I've got plenty.'

Okay, now you can say 'gift horse' and all that, but I wasn't goin' to turn down that offer. In the middle of the friggin' night, wet right through, makin' a rumpus in the old lady's marsh… So I let the kid pour some of that weird tobacco of his into my hat, and then let him slink off across the marsh.

Well, the stuff wasn't exactly Prince Albert, but what the hell, I stuffed it into my pipe, ducked down outa that foolish east wind and lit up.

And you know, about ten minutes and things in the marsh started to seem pretty goddam peachy. I mean, you still couldn't see the stub of your nose, and there's never anything too comfy about an east wind in November, so maybe it was the whiskey and some anticipation about the geese, but god-*dam*, I was feelin' just fine about the entire proceedings.

In fact, I was feelin' so good about it, and about the kid lurkin' around over near to the old lady's joint, that I started to chuckle about it. No, I'm not talkin' about some foolish feeding call — I mean I was laughin' to myself in the marsh. And I can't remember a time before or since when I've pulled that stunt.

But, I'll tell you it was a way to pass the time. I mean, when was the last time you set up for geese at two o'clock in the *A.M.* Huh? Answer me that one, why don't you.

Well, the kid musta had a heavy hand when he loaned me some of his tobacco, 'cause there was a couple of pipefuls in my hat, and they carried me right through to where there started to be a hint of the comin' dawn over the old lady's house.

And as soon as you could see a little, there were the geese. Lord, you should of seen them rafted out there. Hundreds. Thousands maybe. It looked like an early migration. Just gettin' sight of 'em got me gigglin' again — I never had the giggles like that, I mean real schoolgirl stuff — and pretty soon I had to stifle it some because the birds started to move a little out there, lookin' kinda anxious, you know.

And just then, I caught sight of the kid. Right over there under the old lady's nose. I couldn't see the canoe, but there was the kid, all right, and his dog, crouched down straight over on the other side of the geese. God, maybe the deal was goin' to work, I thought.

That shows you what I knew, don't it?

Well, it was about two minutes to shootin' light. I mean, shootin' light for that deal, 'cause the angle is to get the hell out after the poppin's done, and I start fumblin' around for my gun, when goddam it if the kid don't stand up over there. He *stands up*, for Christ sake, and the geese haven't even started to talk it up yet. You know how you can tell when they're goin' to go 'cause they get to honk-arguin' about it first, and that noise hadn't even started yet.

So I got to admit that it took me back when the kid stood up and started pointin' at me. I just couldn't figure it out. I mean it was so strange that I started to laugh about it. I still had those giggles, you know, and — get this, 'cause this'll show you — I stood up and waved back.

'Ah HA!' comes this cackly, godawful witch's voice from behind me. The old lady! She was right behind me! I swiveled around and there she was, standin' on the high ground, pointin' at me like the finger of doom itself.

And then all, I mean *all* the geese got up outa the marsh. You can't imagine the noise they made. You just can't imagine it.

I swiveled around again, back to the marsh, but I got to tell you that my legs had lost the battle. Down I went, ass over teakettle, gun barrels-first into about two feet of marsh muck, and scramblin' to keep my whole self from slidin' down into the creek. And all through it I can hear the old lady goin' 'Ah-ha! Ah-ha!' I was so turned around I didn't know which end was up, and as I'm grabbin' for the marsh grass I catch a glimpse across the marsh. Just a glimpse.

I'll never forget it.

There's the kid, away across the marsh, standin' out stark, gun up and drawin' a bead on the geese.

Blam! Blam! Blam!

And just like that, I tell you, there's three dead geese in the air, comin' down around the kid like rats off a sinking ship. And out comes that dog, takin' a line on the first one hit before it's even in the friggin' water. I'm guessing that he made the triple retrieve just fine. Guessing, that is, because before I can see how he does, those ah-ha's started gettin' louder, and a lot closer. I turn around and here she *comes*. Christ. There was nothin' for it but to swim. I mean, I knew that the old lady wasn't up for a few strokes across Tern Creek at mid-tide, so I just grabbed the old double-gun and belly-whomped into the wet stuff. Jesus, that's a number they wouldn't even pull at Parris Island, and you can count on me not ever, I mean *ever*, doin' that again, but I got over to the other side and cut out up through the cat-briars, headin' for the road. I made it, too, I'm tellin' you, but not until I'd hid out in a drainage ditch for three friggin' hours while the old lady went ragin' all over hell, screamin' 'Ah-ha, ah-ha!'

until I thought she was goin' to attract crows. Christ, what a nightmare.

The older man pours half a tumbler of whiskey for himself and drinks half of it in two swallows before going on.

That's about all there is to it except for the one thing. The one thing… You see, by the time I got here to the house, of course the kid and his dog and his Scout were gone. Long friggin' gone. But right here on this table, laid

out pretty as they come was one a' them geese. Just one. Last one I'll get outa that marsh, I guess.

But what about that kid, huh? What about a kid that does all that? I mean what the hell, it's just too friggin' hard to figure. Who the hell was he? Huh?

Goddam if I'll know it, I guess. But that's the story. That's how it happened, alright.

The older man puts the rest of the whiskey to his mouth, but before he can drink it, the other, the younger man speaks for the first time, quietly:

Tell me. The goose that the kid left behind…

A spattering of wind-driven snow against the glass, a falling of spent logs in the woodstove.

Was it cooked?

Chapter Thirteen

Shooting Light

The light was beginning to go west. Across the marsh the spartina grass had taken on added definition as the lowered sun etched shadows on the autumn-blanched blades and the dropping wind let them stand stiller, ever stiller.

Alone in his hide, the gunner hunched down in a little salt creek run-out. Three feet wide and five deep, it meandered for only another five yards before opening up into the wider slough that could carry small boats in the summer.

But not now.

Now there were salt ice cakes lying on the rich low-tide mud, and the fading afternoon wind carried a winter bite that the shirtless August boaters knew nothing about. With the bluewings, they'd left by Labor Day. Three weeks later the black ducks began to arrive.

Fifteen years and two dogs ago, the

gunner had joined them, bringing his young retriever out onto the marsh on late September evenings to sit quietly by the creek while the black ducks came in. The birds would come down out of the purple gloom to slide by on cupped wings against the orange horizon and the retriever would whine and tense, glued to each passing bird with those brown eyes literally blazing in the reflected western sky.

Steady, boy. Steady. We're just here to look now.

And then later, in season, the two had come back onto the pre-dawn marsh to sit and wait for the morning flight, for the inland-bound black ducks to get up from the estuary and fly overhead. The first birds to fly would get up quacking before shooting time and flit overhead like bats with faint wing-whistles. A pair, usually. And then more and more birds would leave, passing near and far over the gunner's side of the marsh, still too soon.

No light, faint light, shooting light, legal light. Always the sequence. Always the question.

Now?

Not quite.

Black ducks in the air again, and the gunner looking hard. He knew the rule well: If you could see the white underwings, if the bird had dimension beyond pure silhouette, then you could shoot. It worked better than a clock, and he had held to it, even if the dull thumps from another marsh told him that somebody else had decided it was time.

Time was time. And in a morning shoot, the light had no choice but to get better. Light was light.

An evening shoot was different. Darker and darker, and the birds coming in after, it was a closed-end situation and the gunner never liked it. Better the open promise of daybreak than the closing record of nightfall.

Larry had told him of the time he'd come off the big Boston Harbor mudflats just at dark, and how he'd seen the "duskers" heading out: shadowy silent figures moving onto the flats to poach black ducks after dark, shooting at duck shapes in the dim afterglow, and even against the rising moon as the birds came into the sanctuary of the nighttime harbor. You could see their muzzle flashes in the dark.

Steady, boys. Steady.

Sure.

And as he sat alone now in the late afternoon of this season, bent down in the old tidal creek, he could see the passage of it, clearly laid out behind him. His dog now was a setter with three Octobers-full of upland birds and tailgates, old apples and quivering points. That dog had never been

on a salt marsh.

The dark was coming, he could see it. And a black duck would come, he could feel it. But the question was the question, and the answer, he knew, would come in the dark.

Legal light.

Shooting light.

Faint light…